Contents

KU-575-743

Matthew gets £2	4
He could buy a comic ...	6
He could buy some paints ...	8
Matthew spends his money	10
Ottilie's birthday	12
A pen set or a game?	14
Ottilie buys something	16
Arran saves £15	18
An electric car or a football?	20
Arran makes his choice	22
Word bank	24

Matthew's grandad gave him some money.

8

11

To Ottilie

have a **great time!**

Happy Birthday

Love from

Auntie Laura's family

x x x

happy birthday

Ottilie got £5 for her birthday.

12

15

Arran has saved £15
- a ten pound note
and five coins.

20

Sir Arran
the knight.

Word bank

Look back for these words and pictures.

Book

Change

Coins

Electric car

Game

Money

Note

Paints

Saved

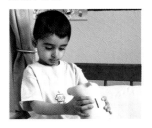

My
Money

Paul Humphrey

Photography by Chris Fairclough

W
FRANKLIN WATTS
LONDON • SYDNEY

First published in 2005 by
Franklin Watts
96 Leonard Street
London EC2A 4XD

Franklin Watts Australia
Level 17/207 Kent Street
Sydney NSW 2000

© 2005 Franklin Watts

ISBN 0 7496 6179 8 (hbk)
ISBN 0 7496 6191 7 (pbk)

Dewey classification number: 332.4

A CIP catalogue record for this book is available
from the British Library.

Planning and production by Discovery Books Limited
Editor: Rachel Tisdale
Designer: Ian Winton
Photography: Chris Fairclough
Series advisors: Diana Bentley MA and Dee Reid MA,
Fellows of Oxford Brookes University

The author, packager and publisher would like to thank the following
people for their participation in this book: Arrandeep and Suki Bola,
Ottilie and Penny Austin-Baker, Matthew and Julie Morris and family,
W & C. A. Griffiths garage, Leintwardine, W. H. Smith, Woolworths.

Printed in China